***

BOOK BEAR

PUBLICATIONS

ABOUT NEAL ABBOTT
"COMPOSING CLASSICS IN OUR TIME"

NOVELS BY NEAL ABBOTT
BloodOrange Sunset
Drover
Prince
Firmament
Pietas

NON-FICTION BY NEAL ABBOTT
My Plans For World Domination
Think Like A Writer
The Gatsby Reader

BLOGWORK BY NEAL ABBOTT
Content Editor for the Creative Writing blog **A WORD FITLY SPOKEN**

The Gatsby Reader

An analysis of *The Great Gatsby*

Neal Abbott

"But his heart was in a constant, turbulent riot. The most grotesque and fantastic conceits haunted him in his bed at night. A universe of ineffable gaudiness spun itself out of his brain while the clock ticked on the wash-stand and the moon soaked with wet light his tangled clothes upon the floor."

BOOK BEAR PUBLICATIONS

□□□□□□□□ □ □□□□ □□□□□

Published by Book Bear Publications 2014
Printed and Distributed by CreateSpace 2014

ISBN-13: 978-1499549591

Table of Contents

Part One: The Narratorship of Nick Carraway

The World Of Nick Carraway

F. Scott Fitzgerald's *The Great Gatsby* is considered by many to be *the* great American novel.[i] Even though the tale regards the doomed love affair of Jay Gatsby and Daisy Faye Buchanan, the book is as much about the narrator, Nick Carraway, as is it about the enamored pair.

Nick, who happens to be Gatsby's neighbor and Daisy's second-cousin, inserts himself into the account by the way he tells the story. As heavy as his presence is, he is only the narrator. Fitzgerald is still the author, and he pulls Nick's strings.

In other words, Fitzgerald uses Nick, not just as the character to tell the tale, but as a particular kind of narrator to say something about the story and to provide a sub-text the reader needs to understand.

But as it is always the problem of sub-text, the author is reliant upon the perceptive skills of the reader. No writer can stand over the shoulder of those who reads his book and offer his own commentary and explanations.

Before he wrote *The Great Gatsby*, Fitzgerald declares that he wants to write something new, beautiful, simple, and intricate.

These last two seem to contradict, so much so that most see the simplicity in the novel and ignore the intricacy.

Even Fitzgerald laments that no one seems to understand *The Great Gatsby*. It may be this ignored intricacy he wished would be noticed. I believe that this is the sub-text that comes from the narratorship of Nick Carraway.

Fitzgerald writes *The Great Gatsby* as a contemporary novel for his own time. It is set in 1922 and written in 1924. The Boom of the Jazz Age was a post-war party. It was a decade Fitzgerald called the world's biggest orgy, and it ended with the Depression. G.I. Joe came home from Europe and danced with his girlfriend, maybe his wife, but ended up having to pay the band more than he could afford.

The world in which Fitzgerald lived is the same world he writes about existing on Long Island. Most have thus labeled *The Great Gatsby* as a commentary of the excess of the Twenties and the death of the American Dream. While this may be a layer, it must be much more than that.

The let-loose of this decade exchanged homecoming for virtue. Nick is thus a narrator set in a world of dissipation. It is not strange then if Nick is himself immoral. Nick's struggles with telling the truth, which forces the reader to scrutinize everything he says as narrator and judge it as truth or error. This is done intentionally by Fitzgerald, hence his intricacy.

The Reliability Of Nick Carraway

Nick Carraway is a liar. That is not uncommon, but it comes into play in that Nick is the narrator of *The Great Gatsby*. This makes the storytelling problematic. But to accuse someone of dishonesty cannot be done lightly, even if it someone who doesn't really exists. Such a charge must be proven or it becomes nothing more than pointless slander.

Examples of Lying

The novel begins by Nick insisting that he was "inclined to reserve all judgments" (5), and then spends the remainder of the book forming judgments of all the other characters.

- ➢ Tom is crude
- ➢ Daisy is shallow
- ➢ Jordan is dishonest
- ➢ George is spiritless
- ➢ Myrtle is sensual
- ➢ Catherine is worldly
- ➢ Mr. McKee is feminine

Whether his judgments are accurate does not matter. It simply manifests his basic dishonesty because he continually practices differently than he preaches.

Most of his judgments have to do with Gatsby himself. These are judgments that swing wildly from one end of the continuum to the other regarding approval and disapproval.[ii]

> Gatsby "represented everything for which I had an unaffected scorn" (7)
> "There was something gorgeous about him" (7)
> "Gatsby turned out all right in the end" (7)
> "An elegant young rough neck" (53)
> "I suspected he was pulling my leg" (70)
> "He was running down like an overwound clock" (97)
> "You're worth the whole damn bunch put together" (162)
> "I disapproved of him from beginning to end" (162)

Nick's lies begin even before we get to any other characters, but with his relations to fellow Yalemen while in school, and particularly as it relates to his false claim to reserve judgments. Because he was sought for council Nick becomes the "victim of not a few veteran bores" (5). He concludes this section by observing that "a sense of fundamental decencies is parceled out unequally at birth" (6). These are both the kinds of judgments he asserts never to have made.

When dealing with these bores at college, Nick confesses that he "frequently … feigned sleep, preoccupations or a hostile levity" (5). To pretend to be asleep, busy or irritated is dishonest. In an interesting confession, Fitzgerald gives a clue to Nick's true nature. Speaking of other men, Nick says, "the intimate revelations of young men or at least the terms in which they express them are usually plagiaristic and marred with obvious suppressions" (6). Nick is still a young man, and so with this, Fitzgerald is cluing us in on Nick's intimate revelation, which is his role as narrator. His story is plagiaristic and marred with obvious suppressions. In other words, Nick is clearly a liar, particularly as the narrator of *The Great Gatsby*.

This begins with the intimate revelation of his own background. He says, "My family have been prominent, well-to-do people in the middle-western town for three generations" (7). Despite this claim, his father can only afford to support him for one year (7). And when the Buchanans ask Nick about the rumor of his engagement, he asserts that he is too poor to marry (24).

He notes that his family claims Scottish nobility, but the reality is that his grandfather's brother, the one responsible for his family line, immigrated here in 1851 and sent a substitute to the Civil War (7). Simply put, immigrants aren't noble, or they'd remain in the old country. And as Nick is supposed to look like this ancestor, he acts like him as well by sending a substitute tale in place of the truth.

The family history is built on dishonesty. During that disconcerting ride with Gatsby to the Manhattan for lunch, Gatsby claims to have gone to Oxford with a young man in a photo who is now the Earl of Doncaster (71). This is a noble title that also belongs to the Duke of Buccleuch, the alleged ancestor of Nick. Since so much of this conversation is false, which we shall soon discover, it is just as likely that this is false, and even inserted merely in Nick's retelling.

When confronted with Nick's basic untruthfulness, some may recall that Nick says about himself, "I am one of the few honest people I have known" (64). Nick Carraway insisting he is honest is like Quinten Compson claiming that he does not hate the South. You an almost bank on the opposite being true.

Think of the stereotypical used car salesman who carries "honest" as a nickname. Just as you wouldn't rely upon *Honest Jake, the Used Car Salesman you can Trust*, no one should believe that Nick is honest just because he says so. If anything, this should be a red flag that makes us wary of anything he says.[iii]

The Drive to Lunch

The drive from Long Island to Manhattan is the hinge of veracity upon which the entire book swings. This passage tells us that not only is Jay Gatsby a liar, but so is Nick Carraway. Gatsby tells Nick his life story so that he will not fall for any of the false rumors going on about him (69) Gatsby makes several claims about himself.

➤ Gatsby comes from a wealthy Midwestern family
➤ All of his family is dead
➤ He was educated at Oxford
➤ His ancestors were educated there

Nick eventually claims to believe all to this, even though he doubts it as it is being told. The most incredible part of this exchange is when Nick asks Gatsby what part of the Midwest he comes from. Gatsby answers, "San Francisco," to which Nick simply replies, "I see" (70).[iv]

Nick's response is more bizarre than Gatsby's answer. Not only is San Francisco not in the Midwest, but Nick never challenges this remark. It is as if Gatsby is saying that all of his claims are as true as San Francisco is a Midwestern town.[v] Nick's response is his agreement to go along with the lie. Gatsby has his story which is just as real as his name, one sprung from his own Platonic conception of himself. Our narrator Nick has agreed to be his accomplice.[vi]

The individual claims Gatsby affirms regarding himself are easy to dissect. First, he says he came from a wealthy family. This is as much a lie as when Nick says the same thing about himself. When Gatsby shows Nick his house, he tells him that it took three years to earn the money to buy the house (95), which may be true, but contradicts his claims of inheriting his wealth. Nick asks about this seeming contradiction.

The problem with lies is the difficulty of consistency, and here Gatsby is caught in a lie, which he tries to explain away. Gatsby says he did inherit money but lost in the big panic of the war, whatever that means. He says that he owned drug stores, but doesn't now (95).

In the days of prohibition grain alcohol was sold over the counter, supposedly medicinally, at certain kinds of drug stores. This seems to be the kind of stores Gatsby owned, which makes him nothing more than bootlegger, just as Tom claims.

Nick's willingness, even his eagerness, to lie on behalf of Gatsby is evident in one particular paragraph. In an attempt to lump all of the rumor together about Gatsby and tell the reader to forget them all, Nick starts with, "He's a bootlegger" (65). Two things stand out about this claim. First of all, it's true. Second of all, no one ever claimed this about him.

Nick moves on to one of claims of Gatsby's past, but packages it in idiocy as if to say the claim is absurd. He notes, "One time he killed a man who found out that he was nephew to von Hindenburg and second cousin to the devil" (65). Nick intentionally lumps the truth of his bootlegging with the clear error of his German political ties.

Instead of being wealthy, Gatsby's folks were "shiftless and unsuccessful farm people" (104). Nick meets his father, Henry Gatz, just before the funeral. Not only is he not wealthy, but he is also not dead, even though Gatsby said as much. Despite this, Nick lies and tells Henry, "He never told me definitely that his parent were dead" (172).

Gatsby's claims about college seem to be some of the most interesting as they play out in the book. He chokes on "educated at Oxford" like the phrase bothers him (69). It should bother him, seeing that he did not even spend two full semesters there. When

Tom confronts him on his Oxford education, Gatsby says, "I only stayed five months. That's why I really can't call myself an Oxford man" (136).

Nick seems to see some sort of verification in this remark, when the reader sees more obfuscation. While he truthfully tells Tom that this technicality is why he cannot call himself an Oxford man, it hasn't stopped him from claiming that before.

Among all the rumors regarding Gatsby, rumors that begin with "I heard" or some sort of qualifier, Jordan says, "He told me once he was an Oxford man" (53). Unless Jordan also deserves to be branded a liar, when she seems to be the truthful foil to Nick, this shows Gatsby to be the one who lied to her. Also, Meyer tells Nick, "He's an Oggsford man" (76). Clearly, he heard Gatsby make the same claim that Jordan did, which shows Gatsby to be a complete liar, and Nick his complicit promoter.

That drive to the city is important for a few reasons. Not only is Nick introduced to Meyer and informed about the subject of an afternoon tea with Jordan, Nick is initiated into a world of duplicity Gatsby had been living with for the past few years. Gatsby lies to Nick, let him know it was a lie, and Nick agrees to repeat the lie with a simple "I see." This is based on more than Nick's general dishonesty, but he has his reasons that are all his own.

The Relationships of Nick Carraway

Understanding literary sub-text involves seeing what is clearly written that is not explicitly written. Fitzgerald leaves us plenty of sub-text regarding Nick Carraway and his relationships. More to the point, Fitzgerald leaves the verbal breadcrumbs for the reader to follow and understand that Nick is homosexual, or at least, bisexual.

This bears on his basic narratorship and how the reader perceives the telling of the story. Some of the exposition may approach bawdiness, which I do not intend, but is necessary for making the case. Also, this is not Fitzgerald composing this simply to be titillating, but for reasons that have to do with the story.

Suggestive Evidence

The manner in which Nick describes men is odd for someone entirely heterosexual. Take as an account Nick's pictures of Tom. When he goes to the Buchanans for dinner and Tom had been riding his horse, Nick comments on Tom's "effeminate swank of his riding clothes" (11).

Nick adds to this how Tom "seemed to fill those glistening boots" (11). Fitzgerald plays on the notion of the size of a man's feet and its indication of his endowment. This is something a man

9

shouldn't be thinking about another man. Further, Nick says, "you could see a great pack of muscles shifting" (11).

At dinner with the Buchanans and Jordan, Daisy tells Nick, "You remind me of a – of a rose, an absolute rose" (19). A rose has often symbolized a female reproductive organ. This is Fitzgerald's attempt to hint at Nick's lack of true masculinity.

At one point Nick says he is lonely and can sense loneliness in others. The example he gives is clerks who must dine alone (62). It seems Nick likes to seek out lonely men and relieve their isolation. Nick tells us of himself as he faces a new decade of living: "Thirty – the decade of a promise of loneliness, a thinning list of single men to know" (143). A heterosexual man would think about the list of single women.

And then there's Gatsby, of whom he says, "there was something gorgeous about him" (6). Men do not call other men "gorgeous," especially at this time.

Something A Bit More Explicit

The closest thing the reader has to a "smoking gun," so to speak, is Nick's "lunch" with Mr. McKee. Note that Nick describes him as a feminine man, not as an effeminate man (34). To call a male a feminine man is to call him a homosexual. That is beyond dispute.

After the party at Tom and Myrtle's apartment, Nick and McKee share an elevator where McKee asks Nick to join him some time for lunch. After this, the elevator operator asks McKee to keep his hands off the lever, and McKee feigns ignorance of having touched it. We don't know explicitly what he was doing with it. But we do know that he is doing something with his hand on this lever, a clear phallic symbol.

The very next sentence reads, "I was standing beside his bed and he was sitting up between the sheets, clad in his underwear, with a great portfolio in his hands" (42). There are two men in a bedroom. One is standing beside the bed (no mention of his dress) and the other in lying in the bed in his underwear. It seems this lunch was nothing more than a homosexual encounter.

Nick's Women

Some may wonder about the apparent women in Nick's life, and if that extenuates anything. Keep in mind that being with a woman is not proof one is not homosexual. Remember that McKee was married. Also the claim about Nick's sexuality is that he is homosexual or bisexual. But even his relationships with women prove odd upon closer examination.

First of all, there is a girl back in Louisville. When the Buchanans ask if Nick were engaged, he denies it, calling it a libel (24). A libel is more than an untruth. It is to claim something about someone that is false because it cannot be true, and runs counter to the nature of that person. Typically a libel is also considered derogatory. There is something about Nick's nature that he cannot marry a woman, and for anyone to claim such is thought of by Nick as almost an insult.

The Buchanans insisted that they heard the rumors and thought them reliable. After lying about having any knowledge about what they were saying, Nick says, "Of course I knew what they were referring to, but I wasn't even vaguely engaged. The fact that gossip had published the banns was one of the reasons I had come east" (24). Nick seems almost repulsed by the notion of marriage to a woman. Later in the novel, Nick says he must write a letter to this girl, and his reason is clear: "there was a vague understanding that had to be tactfully broken off before I was free" (64).

11

There was the brief relationship with an office girl from Jersey City, as well as imagined affairs with strange women, (61). but these amount to nothing either way. The main woman in Nick's life during the summer of 1922 is Jordan Baker. A good look at how Nick sees her does not deny his homosexuality, but rather highlights it.

When Nick first meets Jordan, he says of her, "She was a slender, small-breasted girl with an erect carriage which she accentuated by throwing her body backward at the shoulders like a young cadet" (15). It sounds like he's describing a young man or teenage boy, even adding an odd cadet reference. If Nick were ever attracted to Jordan, it's because she reminds him of a guy.

Even their attempt at romance fell short.

- "She held my hand impersonally" (47)
- Later at the same party Nick lost Jordan, but found her again, and he was glad to go with her since she was well known (62)
- He wasn't in love, but felt a tender curiosity (62)
- "She had deliberately shifted our relations, and for a moment I thought I loved her" (63)
- "Unlike Gatsby and Tom Buchanan I had no girl whose disembodied face floated along the dark cornices blinding signs and so I drew up the girl beside me, tightening my arms" (85)
- In Nick she met another careless driver, and she rebukes him for not being honest and straightforward with her (186)
- Nick clearly was not honest with Jordan concerning his homosexuality. Nick replies to Jordan, "I'm five years too old to lie to myself and call it honor" (186)

These texts demonstrate two people who had the potential to become a couple. Nick seems to come close, but not close enough, to falling completely for Jordan. All they have is a relationship of proximity, curiosity, and dishonesty.

The Object Of Nick's Affection

Others have noticed Nick's homosexuality and his lack of reliability as a narrator. But I have yet to observe any scholar or commentator combine these two ideas. Nick Carraway is dishonest because he is homosexual.

Note that I am not saying all homosexuals are lairs. Nick in general has been shown to be a liar. But it already been pointed out that Nick has agreed to be Gatsby's propagator.[vii] The reason Nick agrees to lie on behalf of Gatsby is because he is in love with him, and by this he colors the tale to protect Gatsby.

Remember that in the beginning Nick says about Gatsby that "there was something gorgeous about him" (6). Nick could have been impressed with what Gatsby has done with himself, or he could have just fallen for his good looks, much the way Daisy did.

Nick remarks that, "Almost any exhibition of self-sufficiency draws a stunned tribute from me" (13). Gatsby exemplifies self-sufficiency if ever one did. But it could have been something more basic and sensual. Nick agrees with Wolfshiem's statement Gatsby is "Handsome to look at and a perfect gentleman" (76).

Even on the ride to the city for lunch with Wolfshiem while Gatsby is spinning his yarn for Nick, he finds it hard to swallow. But something that might have coerced him to agree was the way Gatsby looks. Nick says, "For a moment I suspected he was pulling my leg but a glance at him convinced me otherwise" (70). Notice that it wasn't the evidence that convinced Nick, but looking at Gatsby.

The closest thing Nick gets to a declaration of his feelings for Gatsby is near the end when he tells his neighbor, "You're worth the whole damn bunch put together" (162). Regardless of whether Nick ever had a romantic relationship with a woman, he evinces enough signs of homosexuality, either latent or expressed, to make the reader wonder if his unreliable narratorship has anything to do with it. Nick clearly lies on behalf of Gatsby, and it seems apparent that has a passion and compassion for him that compels to act as he does in telling the story.

Who Killed Myrtle Wilson?

If we are going to believe that Nick lies on behalf of Gatsby, then there had better be some important falsehoods or else Fitzgerald is wasting a perfectly good tool. I argue that there are two great lies Nick tells to protect Gatsby. The first one is that Gatsby drove the so-called "death car" that killed Myrtle Wilson.

The Night Of The Accident

Gatsby tells Nick about what happened, Gatsby begins by saying he drove, which is true. But when he pauses, Nick asks if Daisy drove and Gatsby confirms this, at least, according to Nick the narrator.

The story doesn't make sense. Gatsby supposedly says that he let Daisy drive his car to calm her down. Today we have luxury cars, but the vehicles of the '20s were difficult to drive. Gatsby admits he drove after the accident. If driving is such a balm to the nerves, then he should have let Daisy continue to drive.

Also, he tells Nick that he is hanging around the Buchanan place in case Tom gives Daisy any trouble about the afternoon. More than likely he watches to see if Tom will come after him. If Daisy actually did drive the death car, she never let Tom know. He did not react that night in any manner hostile toward her. When Nick runs into Tom in October, Tom gets it right when he says, "He ran over Myrtle like you'd run over a dog and never even stopped his car" (187).

15

More Than A Hit & Run

Not only did Gatsby drive the death car, it is arguable that it wasn't an accident. While driving through the Valley of Ashes on their way into the city, Gatsby and Nick pass Wilson's Garage. Myrtle is standing outside as they pass. Nick says, "I had a glimpse of Mrs. Wilson at the garage pump with panting vitality as we went by" (72).

This gives Nick the perfect opportunity to tell Gatsby about the woman they just passed and the affair she is having with his second-cousin's husband. Clearly Gatsby knew all about Tom and Myrtle. Outside of the Buchanans, Gatsby tells Nick, "He might think he saw a connection in it" (152).

This remark is absurd if Gatsby knew nothing about Myrtle. But also this is Fitzgerald's way of letting us know that there was some sort of connection. It wasn't Daisy going after her husband's mistress, but Gatsby, who blames Tom for taking Daisy from him, taking Myrtle away from Tom.

Fitzgerald's Foreshadowing

The notion that Gatsby drove the death car is brilliantly foreshadowed earlier in the novel. After the first party, a car drives into the ditch and loses a wheel. The owl-eyed man gets out of the car and insists he knows nothing about driving. He is rebuked for driving when he obviously shouldn't have. Owl-eyes responds, "I wasn't driving. There's another man in the car" (59).

This is Fitzgerald letting us all know that there will be another automobile accident where the driver will be a matter of mistaken identity. This is referring to the mistake of thinking Daisy drove the death car just because Gatsby says she did, or more to the point, narrator Nick claims that Gatsby says she did.

Who Shot Jay Gatsby?

Nick's second lie has to do with Gatsby's death itself. Even after his death, Nick is trying to do the best he can to protect Gatsby's reputation by how he reports his murder. Anyone would agree that to be killed by some madman is less of a scandal than to be assassinated by a gangster. Gatsby was not shot by George Wilson, but by Meyer Wolfshiem, or more than likely, on his orders.

The Circumstances

We are asked to believe the following set of circumstances if we are to hold that George shot Gatsby.

- George owns a garage, but is too poor to own a car, and yet he owns a gun
- He is mentally and physically exhausted from the tragedy of the night before
- He walks many miles over several hours
- After this long walk following a sleepless night, George is composed enough to shoot with a clear eye and a steady hand
- He is such an expert marksman that he can shoot Gatsby while floating on an air mattress upon his pool and never puncture the mattress
- Such trauma would leave only a thin red circle of blood in the water

It is more likely Wolfshiem gave the order for the servants to kill Gatsby. They assassinated him elsewhere and placed his body on the pool air mattress. George stumbles upon this grizzly scene and is then shot since he is a witness. He is then made an easily available patsy.[viii]

The police left the case in its simplest form (171). They probably knew of Wolfshiem's involvement. Nick lets us know that the cops are crooked. When Gatsby is pulled over, the policeman lets him go by simply showing a card (72-73). The card had to do with a favor Gatsby once did for the Commissioner, one that might have involved Wolfshiem's influence.

The Assassin

Wolfshiem himself is an interesting character. He tells the story of a friend of his named Rosy who was assassinated outside of the Metropole. Wolfshiem says he warned Rosy not to go outside, but he did anyway.

During all of this, Wolfshiem makes the most absurd remark: "It was four o'clock in the morning then and if we'd of raised the blinds we'd of seen daylight" (75). This is along the lines of San Francisco being in the Midwest, and is a clue that what he says is untrue. It seems clear that Rosy died at the orders of Wolfshiem, but he retells it as is best for his dead friend.

As Nick and Gatsby talk about Wolfshiem and his involvement in fixing the 1919 World Series, Nick asks why he hasn't been arrested yet. Gatsby replies, "They can't get him, old sport. He's a smart man" (78). It seems Wolfshiem knows how to get involved in criminal activity without ever being bothered by the police. This might explain why Wolfshiem did not want to attend Gatsby's funeral. He does not want any further possible link between himself and his former associate and friend, Jay Gatsby.[ix]

18

Wolfshiem's Reasons

Gatsby is involved in a side hustle involving bonds. Gatsby invites Nick to get in on it and make a bit more money, but Nick refuses (87-88). Gatsby insists Nick will not have to do any business with Wolfshiem, and that the bond scam is confidential.

The hustle falls apart and different players are arrested. All this happens just around the time that Gatsby dies. It's interested that this is a hustle that does not involve Wolfshiem, even though Wolfshiem himself lets Nick know that he and Gatsby always work together (179).[x]

Apparently, Gatsby was branching out on his own, and the attempt failed. Possibly it failed because Wolfshiem was not involved. Regardless, Wolfshiem would rather risk a hit than an investigation into Gatsby's affairs, an investigation that would likely expose Wolfshiem to all sorts of illegalities.

Gatsby's New Servants

Gatsby replaced his servants with Wolfshiem's people to prevent gossip of Daisy's visits. At least that is what he tells Nick. Clearly these are not trained domestics but thugs in training.

- ➢ The grocery boy said the kitchen was a pigsty (120)
- ➢ Those in town said they weren't servants (120)
- ➢ The day of shooting there was dust everywhere (154)
- ➢ It was musty and had not been aired for days (154-155)
- ➢ Nick tells us that, "The chauffer, he was one of Wolfshiem's protégés – heard the shots – afterward he could only say that he hadn't thought anything much about them" (169)

Two things are very clear: George could not have shot Gatsby while Wolfshiem could have and gotten away with it. Also, he seems to have his reason for wanting Gatsby gone. Nick tells us what the police pronounced and partakes of the same lie. The police are protecting Wolfshiem, while Nick is defending Gatsby and his reputation.

What Made Gatsby Great?

With a book title like *The Great Gatsby*, readers necessarily want to know what made Gatsby Great. One can almost hear Fitzgerald's title being announced by a circus ringmaster or sideshow barker. There is a clear amount of theatrics to Gatsby, that is for sure.

- ➤ His mansion, fashioned after the Hotel de' Ville in Normandy, (9) is the perfect stage
- ➤ Owl-eyes compares Gatsby to Belasco, a well-known theatre producer at the time (50)
- ➤ Gatsby's parties provided performances (54-55)
- ➤ His beautiful shirts and cool suits are costumes (98, 125)
- ➤ Tom refers to Gatsby's car as a circus wagon (128)
- ➤ Most important, Jay Gatsby is a fictional character whose life is acted out by James Gatz

Beyond the on-page drama, Nick's very active role as narrator contributes to this greatness. Even though Fitzgerald is the author, Nick is the immediate story teller. One may even attribute the title to Nick as well as the narrative.

Nick alters and suppresses the real story to make Gatsby emerge as unsullied as possible, which is difficult for what Gatsby does and what happens to him. But beyond these bendings of Nick, there is something grand about the personae of Jay Gatsby, even admirable. These are the things that contribute to Gatsby being Great.

Erasure

But there must be another level to this notion of Gatsby's Greatness. Beyond the theatrical it's hard to see. Jay Gatsby is a liar, a criminal, and an adulterer. It's difficult to call this Great.

The only way we can refer to him as Great is forget everything we know about him. This is clearly what Nick did. Before Nick leaves to go back to Louisville, he notices something unusual about Gatsby's mansion: "On the white steps an obscene word, scrawled by some boy with a piece of brick, stood out clearly in the moonlight and I erased it, drawing my shoe raspingly along the stone" (188).[xi]

This is the only way Nick can conceive of Gatsby as Great. Keep in mind that "Gatsby … represented everything for which I have an unaffected scorn" (6). Yet in spite of this contempt, Nick can say "Gatsby turned out all right in the end" (6). There's something about Gatsby where he cannot be thought of a Great until the end of the story.

Notice that it was just after Nick erased this obscene word that he goes to the beach and has his epiphany about Gatsby and the Dutch sailors. Nick does more than erase one obscene word from a step, he erases all of Gatsby's obscenity, and only then can he think of Gatsby as Great, only then can he turn out all right in the end. And Nick expects us to erase from our minds all of the obscenity we know about Gatsby.

The book is full of images of erasure and vanishing.[xii]

➢ At the first party there are "gins liqueurs and cordials so long forgotten that most of his female guests were too young to know one from another" (44)

- There were "casual innuendos and introductions forgotten on the spot" (44)
- Many of Gatsby's guests never met him (45)
- Nick and Jordan can't find Gatsby (49)
- Owls-eyes says books are real but the pages aren't cut (50)
- Emptiness flowed from windows after the party (60)

Even the many rumors about Gatsby indicate a type of disappearance.

- Gatsby is the Keiser's nephew (37)
- He once killed a man (48)
- He was a German spy (48)
- He served in the American army (48)
- "He's a bootlegger" (65)
- "One time he killed a man who and found out that he was nephew to von Hindenburg and second cousin to the devil" (65)

There is a continual disappearance with Gatsby in particular in regards to Nick.

- Gatsby's smile vanishes as soon as it becomes significant
- "My incredulity was submerged in fascination now; it was like skimming hastily though a dozen magazines" (71)
- "I turned toward Mr. Gatsby, but he was no longer there" (79)
- "Gatsby looked with vacant eyes" (89)
- Nick is reminded of "an elusive rhythm, a fragment of lost words" that he can't say, and when he tries, "they made no sound and what I had almost remembered was uncommuniable forever" (118)

Gatsby himself practices his own type of erasure by attempting to remove the past five years and reuniting a relationship with Daisy Faye, just as he had left it when he departed Louisville and shipped out for Europe to fight in the Great War. He insists to Daisy that one can repeat the past (116).

After Gatsby and Daisy are reunited, Nick thinks about how the green light at the end of the Buchanans's dock will go back to being just a green light and nothing more. He thinks about how "the colossal significance of that light had now vanished forever" (98).

Nick adds that this significance, which once was large, now seems "as close as a star to the moon" (98). Just as the significance of the green light vanishes, so does the new proximity. Their new relationship may seem as close as a star to the moon, but in reality that is a great distance covering hundreds and thousands of millions of miles.

This effort by Gatsby to erase the past five years is wonderfully prefigured in the same scene used to foreshadow Gatsby and the death car, the accident outside of his house after the first party. Even though the wheel is off, the driver wishes to try to drive it to the garage. When other partygoers point out his absurdity, he replies that there is "No harm in trying" (60). Gatsby is trying to drive a car without wheels by trying to take Daisy away from Tom just as the driver wants to erase the entire accident itself.

There are attempts at making things disappear on the hottest day in the summer of '22 and all of the drama that takes place in the Plaza Hotel. Not only is Gatsby practicing erasure, but so are Daisy and Tom in their own ways. Keep in mind the writing genius of Fitzgerald and his subtle use of setting to make an indelible point to the readers. The heat of the day symbolizes hell, the hell everyone is about to go through.

The only escape for Daisy and her own personal hell is Gatsby himself. On this scorching day, Daisy says to Gatsby "You always look so cool" (125). A new hell is about to begin for Tom, as Nick notes, "There is no confusion like the confusion of a simple mind and as we drove away Tom was feeling the hot whips of panic" (131). Tom is beginning to feel the heat, but his advice is simple: "The thing to do is forget about the heat" (133). To Tom, Gatsby is beneath him and someone not to worry about, which is his version of erasure.

Fitzgerald continually uses the image of vanishing and disappearance to underscore Nick's narrative efforts to erase all of Gatsby's obscenity. Only then can Gatsby begin to be considered Great.

White In America

The Great Gatsby was written at a time when racism, nativism, and white supremacism were growing sentiments. It was a time when to be American was to be white, and to be white was to be an American. But this idea of white is more than fair in pigment. It is limited to people from Anglo and Germanic heritages. This leaves out Mediterranean, Slavic, and Baltic countries. Also, this is a white that is Christian, and more specifically, Protestant.

This attitude is seen in certain characters in the novel.

- ➢ Tom promotes the book *The Rise of the Coloured Empires* by Goddard (17)
- ➢ Concerning this book and its subject, Tom says, "It's up to us who are the dominant race to watch out or these other races will have control of things" (17)
- ➢ Catherine says, "I almost made a mistake, too. I almost married a little kyke …. I knew he was below me" (38)
- ➢ Catherine also lies about Daisy being Catholic, but it clearly is an insult (38)
- ➢ In the Plaza hotel room, Jordan comments that "We're all white here" (137)
- ➢ Even Nick tries to secure his Scottish heritage (7)

This racism plays into this notion of erasure in that Gatsby is not white. He is pictured against African-American for comparison, but more than likely, he is Jewish. Nick says that he "would accept without question the information that Gatsby sprang from swamps of Louisiana or lower eastside of New York" (54). These are predominantly non-white parts of this country.

As Gatsby and Nick drive into Manhattan they are passed by a funeral whose mourners appear to be from southeastern Europe. Soon after this they are passed by a white limousine with three modish-dressed blacks. On the tail of these two sights while driving through a non-white portion of New York, Nick feels anything can happen now that they have crossed this bridge. Even Gatsby can happen without any particular wonder (73).

Gatsby can happen in a manner that makes sense to Nick in a non-white part of the city in the surroundings of non-whites. While at lunch, Wolfshiem tells Nick, "I knew I had discovered (in Gatsby) a man of fine breeding" (76). Wolfshiem is Jewish, and for a Jewish man to speak of another's fine breeding implies that the other is Jewish, also.

According to certain characters in this novel, Gatsby is not white and he is not a real American. Tom's fear of the encroaching non-white races symbolizes his dread of losing Daisy to a man like Gatsby. Not only is Gatsby and Daisy's reunification this actual non-white encroachment, it is also an erasure of Gatsby's non-white status.

Just before Nick commits to Gatsby's lie, a lie that has everything to do with winning Daisy back, Nick comments on how Gatsby looks when he comes to pick him up. Nick says, "he was balancing himself on the dashboard of his car with that resourcefulness of movement that is so peculiarly American" (68). Nick is already attempting this racial erasure.

Later as the tea party moves from Nick's house, Nick talks about Gatsby's mansion and its previous owner. After he died his children sold the house with the black wreath still on the door.

Nick's explanation for this is, "Americans, while occasionally willing to be serfs, have always been obstinate about being peasantry" (93).

Nick is saying that Gatsby's pursuit of Daisy, made capital with her reacquisition, is making him American. Gatsby is willing to be Daisy's servant but he is not willing to be poor. In fact, he knows that he cannot have her as long as he is poor. Gatsby's wealth is just a means to the ends of getting back with Daisy. She is his American Dream.

To Answer The Question

What ultimately makes Gatsby so Great is this erasure of his non-whiteness and establishment as an American. Jay Gatsby exists in the clearest way of what it means to be an American. He is an American Everyman.

Nick wonders at Gatsby's capacity for hope. Fitzgerald ties this into the American ideal in his close to the novel. Before Nick leaves West Egg, he looks around and thinks about the wonder that Dutch sailors must have felt when they first saw this New World. This sense of wonder is also expressed as their dreams in this verdant and green world.

Fitzgerald moves then to the green light at the end of the dock of the Buchanan house across the courtesy bay over in East Egg. Remember that the first time Nick sees Gatsby, the playboy is standing on the beach staring at the green light. Fitzgerald ties the Dutch wonder of dreams regarding this new, green republic to Gatsby's hope when he then tells us that "Gatsby always believed in the green light."

In his closing words, Fitzgerald associates all of this with you and I with the personal pronoun "we." The sailors' dreams and

Gatsby's belief symbolize American hope. Just like Gatsby, someday we will reach out further and we will run faster.

This hope of Gatsby's didn't quite work out like he would have liked it. In fact, his hope started after his failure had begun; and still, he hoped. Like the dreamful Gatsby, we beat on, even though our boats run against the current. This is because of what has already been locked in by our past. And yet, we continue to hope.

Americans are indeed the inheritors of these Dutch sailors and all who came to this New World looking for a better life. Scholar comment on how *The Great Gatsby* addresses the failure of the American Dream, and yet, we as Americans still dream. Bunker Hill didn't kill the revolution, it fueled it. The dread of 9/11 did not compel us to give up, but pull together a rebuild. We don't throw in the towel very easily, even when it seems there is every reason to. He is We and We are He, and if Gatsby is Great, then you and I are Great, too.

The Beautiful People

One of the most cherished couples in all of American literature is Daisy Faye Buchanan and Jay Gatsby. Of all the beautiful people one might read, they seem the most adorable. Fitzgerald uses a powerful device to show what makes these people attractive and attracted to each other. Instead of describing many indelible aspects of each, he selects one thing to accentuate and make that beyond spectacular. For Daisy it is her voice, and for Gatsby it is his smile.

Fitzgerald uses Nick the narrator to bring out these aspects for both of these characters. For Daisy it serves as an explanation for why Gatsby fell for her so strongly and worked so diligently to build his wealth to re-obtain her. Regarding Gatsby's appeal, the reader sees why Daisy fell for him, as well as Nick himself.

Daisy's voice
Most of the descriptions are for Daisy's voice, while merely a few describe Gatsby's smile.
  - ➤ Nick refers to "her low, thrilling voice" (13)
  - ➤ "It was the kind of voice that the ear follows up and down as if each speech is an arrangement of notes that will never be played again" (13)

- In Louisville Lt. Gatsby looks at Daisy while she was speaking (80)
- "The exhilarating ripple of her voice was a wild tonic in the rain" (90)
- Just after Gatsby comes in from the rain, Nick says that he hears Gatsby then Daisy's voice on a "clear and artificial note" (91)
- "Her throat (was), full of aching, grieving beauty, (and) told only of her unexpected joy" (94)
- "Daisy's voice was playing murmurous tricks in her throat" (111)
- "Her voice struggled on through the heat, beating against it, moulding it senselessness into forms" (125)
- "She turned to me and her voice, dropping an octave lower, filled the room with thrilling scorn" (139)
- "She had caught a cold which make her voice huskier and more charming than ever" (157)

Daisy's voice is the kind that brings about responses from other people, even if they are unaware of it. Nick says, "Daisy's murmur was only to make people lean toward her" (13). Similarly, he adds, "her voice compelled me forward breathlessly as I listened" (18). Her voice only work when she speaks, so when she is silent, the voice's compelling draw ends. Nick points this out when he says, "The instant her voice broke off, ceasing to compel my attention, my belief, I felt that basic insincerity of what she had said" (22).

On the hottest day of the year, it was "Daisy's voice (that) got us to our feet" (126). It was Daisy's voice that constrains the heart of young Gatsby, both before and after the war. He may have built her up to be more than she is, but her voice that remained as flawless and endearing as it ever was to Gatsby. At their reunion Nick says, "as she said something low in his ear he turned toward her with a rush of emotion. I think that voice held him most with its fluctuating, feverish warmth because it could not be over-dreamed – that voice was a deathless song" (101).

30

Daisy's voice seems to have its limits. It operates on those who have the capacity to truly cherish her, and who in fact practiced this admiration. Nick says, "there was an excitement in her voice that men who had cared for her found difficult to forget" (14).

Her voice stirs Gatsby as well as Nick at the beginning, but there is one key character who seems immune to the serenity of her voice, and that is her husband Tom. He comments that he does not like it when she says "hulking" (16). If her voice works best on men who care for her, and it does not seem to have such sway over Tom as it does others, then the obvious conclusion is that Tom does not care for Daisy.

What made Daisy's voice so compelling is identified in three passages. At the Buchanan dinner Nick says, "a stirring warmth flowed from her as if her heart was trying to come out to you concealed in one of those breathless, thrilling words" (19). Nick points out that it is her heart coming out to you in her words that make her speech do endearing.

Nick also says Daisy's voice contains promises. Particularly the promise that she had done exciting things and there was more to come soon (14). But the most telling feature of Daisy's voice is Gatsby's blunt assertion that she has an indiscreet voice that is full of money (127).

Gatsby's smile

There are fewer references to Gatsby's smile than to Daisy's voice, but those few are powerful. The first and last stands out. We first see the Gatsby grin when he meets Nick at one of the Summer Bacchanals. It was a smile of eternal reassurance, one that was for everyone before it focused on you and made you feel every good thing about yourself you ever wanted felt (52-53). Anyone would like someone to smile at them like that.

The other took place as Nick leaves Gatsby, not knowing it was for the last time. He paid him the only compliment he ever offered, and Gatsby smiled. His smile said that they were always in agreement on the praise just pronounced (162). His smile, like Daisy's voice, seems to be one of special inclusion.

Daisy's voice is always full of hope and promises. For a young Gatsby trying to recreate himself into perfection, this voice bolsters his dreams. Gatsby's smile draws you in and confirms you every confidence and shreds your deepest doubts. Daisy sees her own validation here. While other young men may seek her out because she is wealthy or beautiful, she falls for Gatsby because of a self-assurance she receives form him.

Both Gatsby and Tom are described as restless, and possibly Daisy is drawn to this type. Maybe she is restless, too. This restlessness may be a general lack of contentment and deep search for some validation. In the final analysis, both Gatsby and Daisy are sustained by the other and they pour themselves into the same mould every young couple in love tries to do. Their story ends in death and sadness, yet theirs is a timeless tale of passion that persists even when it seems there is no more reason

Part Two: Gatsby As A Grail Quest

Did Fitzgerald Write A Grail Quest?

High schoolers have been reading F. Scott Fitzgerald's *The Great Gatsby* for decades. Since most sophomores are too, well, sophomoric to appreciate it for the great work of literature that it truly is, they usually leave high school with *The Great Gatsby* as one of many sour tastes left in the mouth. Since most teens hate what they have to read, most don't re-read *Gatsby* once they have become adults.

That is a terrible shame, since it is truly a wonderful book. Despite being not read enough, *The Great Gatsby* remains one of the most familiar stories to date. It has been the subject of five movies and even an opera.

In the first half of this book I wrote on the matter of Nick Carraway as a narrator. This portion will explore Fitzgerald as another writer to tackle the Grail Legend. When we read that the valley of ashes is a Waste Land, or that Gatsby had committed himself to the following of a grail, it seems clear that Fitzgerald intended to intertextually layer his novel with Grail Quest imagery. This requires three particular tasks for the reader: identifying the Grail Knight, the Fisher King, and the Holy Grail.

According To Weston

In 1920, *From Ritual To Romance* by Jessie Weston broke new ground concerning Grail scholarship. Before Weston, academians took one of two positions: Grail lore should be considered strictly as Christian literature or pagan lore. Weston pointed out the strengths of both positions while further demonstrating the insufficiency of either standpoint alone. Her solution is to combine the two.[xiii]

In other words, the panoply of Grail literature is a combination of Christian and pagan sources. In this it is not much different from other medieval works like *Beowulf*. Weston relies heavily Sir James Frazer's *The Golden Bough*. It was published in two volumes in 1890, three in 1990, and a dozen between 1906-1915.

The Maimed King & The Fisher King

Weston explores the pagan roots to the Grail as manifestations of ancient fertility cult. In particular, Grail legends call upon the mysteries of Tammuz, Adonis, and Attis. According to Frazer and Weston, the notion of the king as divine comes from the idea that he represented god. And when god is good for nothing more than providing a bumper crop, fertility cults commonly held the sway of primitives. So with Tammuz, Adonis, and Attis, and as extension, the kings of people who worshipped these idols, their personal health reflected on their ability to provide for the worshippers.

If the king is wounded, then the land is laid waste. So in Grail literature, this becomes the Maimed King who presides over the Waste Land. Based upon the variation, there is also a Fisher King, who is sometimes also the Maimed King, or other times, related to the Maimed King. The image of the fish has often been a symbol of fertility. For example, within the fertility cult of Dagon, the chief deity was pictured as a fish. And thus, the term Fisher King refers to the king as divine who has the power to provide for the livestock and crops of his citizens.

Within Grail writings, the Fisher King and/or Maimed King are more central to the story than the Grail Knights. By obtaining the Grail, the waters are freed, the king is healed, and the land becomes fertile once more. Based upon the individual texts, the king or the knight vary in importance, with the older texts laying more of an emphasis on the king and the more recent stressing the story of the knight. Malory's *Le Morte d'Arthur* does not even mention a Fisher or Maimed King, although their fingerprints are all over the Sangraal section of the book.

The Grail Knights

Gawain, Percival, and Galahad have all been Grail Knights. And while they may have their differences, their role is mostly the same. The Grail Knight is tasked with finding the Holy Grail, the chalice used by Jesus at the Last Supper. Only the pure may obtain it, and finding the Grail is the ultimate of spiritual ascendancy. The success or failure of the Grail Knight has to do with asking, or not asking, the correct questions: *What is the Grail? Whom does it serve?*

Fitzgerald would have been well aware of Weston's work. T.S. Eliot writes in the commentary of his own 1922 poem "The Waste Land" that he leaned heavily on Weston in composing his poem. It is not a stretch to think that Fitzgerald would have learned these things and worked them into his 1925 epic. The issue for the reader is to figure out if this is the case or not. The question is answered by looking at another question: Can I identify the Grail Knight, the Fisher King, and the Holy Grail in *The Great Gatsby*? These matters will be explored throughout the remainder of this book.

Jay Gatsby As Grail Knight

If we are going to explore *The Great Gatsby* as a Grail Quest, one of the first tasks would be to identify the Grail Knight. Fortunately, Fitzgerald has done all of the heavy lifting for us when he tells us that Gatsby found that he had committed himself to the following of a grail (156). It could not be clearer.[xiv]

Also, we know that the glasses in which champagne served at Gatsby's parties was likened to large finger bowls (51). These finger bowls symbolize this same Grail that Gatsby followed. This is Fitzgerald's way of telling the reader how Gatsby pursued this Grail. The parties, like all of Gatsby's possessions, were a means of obtaining Daisy and everything that entailed.

In 1961, W.H. Auden wrote an article called "The Quest Hero." While it largely dealt with *The Lord Of The Ring*, its standards may be used to meter Gatsby as a legitimate Quest hero.[xv] Auden listed the following components as elements of a Quest legend:
- A cherished *Object* or *Person* to be obtained
- A long *Journey* that takes a long time to complete
- A worthy *Hero*
- A *Test* to demonstrate worthiness
- The *Guardians* of the Object who must be overcome
- The *Helpers* of the hero

The Great Gatsby meets all of these benchmarks, and can be considered a matter of Quest lore. Daisy is the cherished person to be obtained, although she is not the Grail. Gatsby's journey took him from Louisville to the European theatre of the Great War, and to Oxford. Eventually Gatsby ends up in Chicago only to move to New York. Here he works for Meyer Wolfshiem bootlegging grain alcohol, and in three years he has the money to buy his mansion on West Egg. All of this in four and half years. Gatsby's worthiness comes about by no other means than his wealth, for that is all he needs to win Daisy.[xvi] The tour of his mansion after the tea party is the test, and he passes with literally flying colors (his shirts).[xvii] Tom is the Guardian to be overcome, while Nick and Jordan are the helpers who aid in arranging the tea party and its reunion.[xviii]

Based upon this, Gatsby is a Quest hero, but so are Odysseus and Jason. But neither of these two Greeks are Grail heroes. This particular story structure rides on a horse of a slightly different color. Not only must there be a legitimate Quest hero, but there must also be a wounded king who presides over a Waste Land, and whose infertility may be cured by the obtaining of the Holy Grail. That puts little more on the plate that our hero needs to eat.

George Wilson As Fisher King

Identifying the Fisher King may be the most difficult of tasks, but in truth, may be one of the most vital in correctly interpreting *The Great Gatsby* as a Grail Quest.[xix] Since the Fisher King is so inexorably tied to the Waste Land, one cannot find one without finding the other. The valley of ashes is the most evident Waste Land.[xx] Even Fitzgerald uses this term to describe the valley of ashes (28). If the valley of ashes is the Waste Land, then the clearest candidate for the Fisher King is George Wilson.

George's Realm

The valley of ashes, which is nothing more than a trash dump for Manhattan and Long Island, has three constructions alongside the road where business is to take place. One is empty with a *For Rent* sign, the second is a restaurant, and the third is Wilson's garage.

The empty facility is a clear symbol of infertility. Michaelis's restaurant is a sick banquet hall. And if a car can be compared to a horse, then Wilson's garage may be comparable to a stable, where Wilson works, lives, and presides over the Waste Land, all under T.J. Ecklesburg's omniscience. The descriptions of Wilson and his garage demonstrate his unproductiveness (29-30). The interior of the garage is unprosperous and bare. The only car in the garage is a dust-covered wreck. Wilson wipes hands on piece of waste. He is a spiritless and anemic man. He mingles with cement color of walls.

All of these infertile images work for George Wilson, but not for his wife, Myrtle. She has a "perceptible vitality." An ashen dust veiled everything but her, and Myrtle walked through George (30). Fitzgerald tells us that George Wilson seemed faintly capable of moving, and he was his wife's man and not his own (145). There was not enough of him for his wife (167). The great differences between George and Myrtle are not incidental, but they have everything to do with the state of the Waste Land itself. In the more ancient of Grail texts, the ruin of the Fisher King's realm is the result of a curse that came about from marrying a pagan princess.

While the valley of ashes serves as a perfect Waste Land, it is not the only one of the book. The true Waste Land spreads from Manhattan to Long Island. And as the valley of ashes is a trash dump, so does it symbolize the moral and spiritual refuge of these two outer lands. In fact, the entire novel describes a Waste Land of these sorts.

> The parties at Tom & Myrtle's apartment as well as the ones at Gatsby's mansion
> Gatsby's crooked bond scheme as well as Nick's legitimate speculative work
> The adulteries of Tom & Myrtle, Gatsby & Daisy
> Jordan's cheating at golf along with Gatsby & Nick's constant lying
> Wolfshiem & Gatsby's bootlegging

Expanding The Border

As the valley of ashes is a place of constant dust, Fitzgerald uses the symbol of dust throughout the novel to describe spiritual and moral barrenness. Near the beginning we read that a foul dust floated in the wake of Gatsby's dreams (6). When Nick reports that there is dust everywhere in Gatsby's mansion since Wolfshiem's people took over domestic roles, we can see the Waste Land that is Gatsby & Daisy's illicit affair (154). Even before Daisy meets Gatsby, her life is spent in a hundred pairs of golden and silver slippers shuffled the shining dust (158), and this dust is the moral corruption of a life spent in the Waste Land.

The party at Tom & Myrtle's apartment uses a different but equally compelling image of infertility. The only item hung on the wall is a portrait that to Nick looks like a hen sitting on rock (33). As eggs have always been symbols of fertility, a hen on a rock reminds us of the bareness of the Waste Land, but also the moral and spiritual sterility of the lives of those people carousing in that apartment, beginning with Tom & Myrtle's adultery.

If George Wilson is the Fisher King in this Grail Quest, it could then be argued that the Wounded King may be T.J. Eckleburg's billboard.[xxi] His eyes represent the eyes of God that can see but can do nothing for these vacuous people. This keenly accents those who try to live a life without God, as George Wilson so wisely says to Michaelis (167-168).

This brings us to his living counterpart, Owl-eyes. We consider owls the harbinger of wisdom, so this character's insights are noteworthy. Owl-eyes notices that all of the books in Gatsby's library are real, but that the pages have not been cut. He refers to Gatsby as a real Belasco, who is a Broadway producer of the 20s (50). Owl-eyes not only lets us all know that everything in the mansion is a set piece for show, he further lets us know of the moral emptiness behind it. Gatsby wants to appear well-read just as he

43

wishes to come across as highly educated by referring to himself as an Oxford man.

After this party there is an automobile wreck and Owl-eyes emerges from the vehicle. The driver of the car wants to drive on to the nearest garage even though the car only has three wheels now (60). This all symbolizes how Gatsby's dreams are as futile as driving a three-wheeled car, but he is willing to do it because his dreams are soiled by the dust of the Waste Land. And it is from these fouled dreams that Gatsby perishes, so it is significant that Owl-eyes is one of three people to attend Gatsby's funeral. The owl is also a death omen as well as a symbol of wisdom, so Owl-eyes's wisdom reminds us that the death of Gatsby is inexorably bound to his depravity.

The Virtue Of George Wilson

If anyone deserves to preside over a prosperous kingdom, it's George Wilson. He is clearly the most ethical and honorable character in the novel. When asked about his work by Tom, George replies that he has no complaints (29), even though he clearly has plenty going wrong that he could complain about. Even though he is sick and is advised to go to bed and rest, George refuses because of the business he may miss out on. One may see a good work ethic here.

George As A Hard Worker

George Wilson is not only a hard worker, but the only person in the novel who does honest work. The Buchannan's are the idle rich. Jordan Baker is a cheating athlete. Gatsby and Wolfshiem are gangsters and criminals. Nick sells bonds on Wall Street at a time when speculation is rampant and will ruin the economy before the decade finishes. Nick could have taken on honest labor, but gave it a pass when he chose not to work in the family hardware store. George comments on how Tom's man works slow (29). This further demonstrates George's strong work ethics. When Tom warns George's that most people will try to cheat you if given the chance,

45

that demonstrates both the projection of his own predisposition to cheat others and George's unwillingness to be anything but fair. Even the dog seller is a cheat (31-32).

George's honorableness may be associated with his own unique level of spirituality. He is the only character who ever refers to God. Maybe living under the constant oversight of Doctor T.J. Ecklesburg's divinely emblematic billboard encourages him to live morally. When George learns of Myrtle's infidelity, he tells her that God sees everything, and that you can't fool God (167). Earlier in the novel when Tom and Nick leave George's garage, Tom says that the garage is a terrible place, and then frowns at the eyeglass billboard (30). To Tom, the eyes of God make it a terrible place, or said in other words, a place that is full of terror. God's all-seeing eyes frighten an immoral man like Tom, but encourage uprightness in a person like George.

George's Healing

After commenting that George's garage is a terrible place, Tom says that George is so dumb he doesn't even know he's alive (30). Tom is not an astute observer of the human scene, so his remarks are immediately suspect. In fact, George is quite smart. Both he and Michaelis witness Myrtle's accident, but only George notices that the man in the car murdered her when she runs out to the car to speak to him (166). Michaelis thinks she is fleeing George and that it is nothing but a terrible accident.

George's constant spirituality makes it possible for him to ascend to a spiritual height no other character is capable of. In a sense, he heals himself of a manner of spiritual barrenness that is typical with the Waste Land. This begins with learning what brought about his curse in the first place: his wife. When he learns of her affair, he shows strength for seemingly the first time in the book by

46

resolving to move out West with his wife. Nick notices that George looks guilty (131). He does not begin with blaming others, but himself possibly for not being a good husband in Myrtle's eyes in the first place. After she is killed and George seeks out the owner of the yellow car, he makes it to the top of Gad's hill on his way to West Egg (168). Another way of saying Gad's hill would be God's hill, or, the mountain of the house of the Lord, figuratively called Zion in the Bible. Ascending God's hill is in contrast to living in the valley of ashes.

The remarkable and tragic aspect of George's role in *The Great Gatsby* is that he is in some small sense redeemed from his curse, but it leads to his death, which some might argue is still being under the curse associated with the Waste Land. If it does seem he is briefly delivered, it does not come about by Gatsby as the Grail Knight obtaining the Holy Grail.

Daisy Faye Buchannan's Role

Some might conclude that if Jay Gatsby is the Grail Knight within *The Great Gatsby*, then Daisy must be the Grail. Consider the high value and precious nature of the Grail. It is the zenith of spiritual perfection and only the most pure may obtain it. When one regards the exalted nature of the Grail, the poor moral quality of Daisy makes her an ill fit Grail candidate.

To make Daisy the Grail would be to degrade the Grail, so another pursuit of Gatsby's needs to be put forth. Still, Daisy has a role in the Grail Quest even though she is not the Grail itself. We get a strong clue is the remark made by Nick that for Gatsby the rock of his world was founded on a fairy's wing (105). The weight of this statement is clear when we recall the ancient word for fairy is fay. Because of the mischievousness of fairies in most ancient lore, fay, or fey, is also a world that means "false." In the Arthurian world of Grail legends, Daisy's maiden name reminds the reader of another character, the wicked sorceress Morgan le Fay.[xxii]

Daisy's Charming Voice
In a previous chapter, the case was made that Daisy's voice is her most attractive and compelling feature. Daisy's voice moved other

49

people to act much like a magician can force things based upon spells that are spoken. Nick says, "Daisy began to sing with the music in a husky, rhythmic whisper, bringing out a meaning in each word that it had never had before and would never have again. When the melody rose her voice broke up sweetly, following it, in a way contralto voices have, and each change tipped out a little of her warm human *magic* in the air" (114-115 – emp. mine, na). Considering Gatsby's insight, Nick further notes that Daisy's voice was full of money, and that is what gave it its *charm* (127 – emp. mine, na). A charming voice can be spellbinding, to say the least.

So when reading *The Great Gatsby* on the level of a Grail Quest, not only is Daisy Faye Buchannan the sorceress, it seems she has enchanted Gatsby with a love spell. It may help explain why he does so many ridiculous things in his pursuit of Daisy. One example may be Gatsby's wardrobe. Any reader of *The Great Gatsby* knows that Gatsby accumulates his wealth to win Daisy back again. Also, that one of the most visible and tangible manifestations of his wealth is his shirts of many colors. In fact, these shirts illicit the strongest emotion from Daisy (97).

Near the end of the book there is another reference to Daisy's charming voice. Although near the end of the book, the incident deals with Daisy and Gatsby's first month together. After noting that Daisy caught a cold and it made her voice more charming that ever, Fitzgerald goes on to say that by this voice Gatsby becomes aware of the freshness of many clothes, amongst other things (157).

Gatsby associates Daisy's appeal, in other words her charm, with her voice. And to Gatsby, Daisy's voice brings an awareness of the freshness of many clothes. So while under Daisy's spell, Gatsby buy many clothes, shirts in particular. These are a part of his wealth, all accumulated as a means of winning back Daisy.[xxiii]

Examples Of Magic

There are episodes and demonstrations throughout the book of Daisy's sorcery. When the Buchanan's, Nick, and Jordan have dinner near the beginning of the novel, Daisy says that it will soon be the longest day of the year and that she wants to plan to do something on that day. She even goes to say she has this thought every year. Every reader of Shakespeare will readily know that the longest day of the year, i.e. Midsummer, is a day associated with magic, lover's dreams, and madness.

The clearest example is when Gatsby and Daisy are reunited at Nick's tea party.

> Gatsby re-evaluates all of his possessions based on Daisy's opinion of them (97)
> He did so again after Myrtle Wilson dies as if the spell is wearing off (169)
> Gatsby stares at his possessions in a dazed way (97)
> He was consumed with wonder at her presence (97)
> While with Daisy, Nick notices an expression of bewilderment on Gatsby's face (101)
> Nick notes that on that day there must have been times where Daisy fell short of the colossal vitality of Gatsby's own illusion (101)

This general bewilderment is no different than when they first met. Just as Gatsby was so under Daisy's spell and she succumbing to his smile back in Louisville so that neither noticed Jordan when she approached (79), so too does the couple fail to pay attention to Nick at their reunion (94,101). And lest any reader forget all about this magical courtship, we are reminded in the closing that Gatsby's sense of hope and wonder regarding Daisy is comparable to the state of *enchantment* once felt by Dutch sailors as they first found New York (189 – emp. mine, na). This enchantment felt at first by the old world mariners and subsequently the platonically-bourne bootlegger reminds us of Gatsby's search for a Grail, as well as Daisy's mystical role in both creating and defeating the Quest.

Identifying The Grail

In the Grail Quest of *The Great Gatsby*, Gatsby is the Grail Knight, but Daisy is not the Holy Grail. The novel reveals that Gatsby pursues something even more strenuously than her, and that is the restoration of the past. This is the Grail, the desire to turn back the clock and stop time. Fitzgerald sets temporal reference throughout the book, such as noting the sun-dials at the Buchannan mansion (11), which mark the progression of time, or how Nick writes the names of Gatsby's guests on time-table (65). Even the end of the novel reminds us of the universal appeal to live one's life against the flow by reaching back into the past (189).

Nick's Tea Party
At the age of seventeen, James Gatz reinvents himself into Jay Gatsby. Fitzgerald writes that it is this platonic conception to which Gatsby would stay faithful (104). This is the first level of his past Gatsby wishes to restore, a time when he sails the world with Dan Cody. But Cody dies, and time goes on.

His heart is always in a turbulent riot (105). It is this riot that he wishes to quiet. The closest he has even come to peace is when he first kisses Daisy Faye. Just before he kisses her, he realizes that once he had kissed her, then "his mind would no longer romp like the mind of God." (117) Gatsby is not primarily interested in having a romantic relationship with Daisy, but in going back to a time of brief contentment and internal comfort.

Gatsby's initial grand gesture to restore this past is moving to West Egg and throwing all of his summer parties. He hopes Daisy might one evening stroll back into his life. Also, Gatsby uses these gatherings to see who knows her. He finds out Jordan Baker knows her and that his neighbor and Jordan's friend Nick is her cousin.

Through Jordan, Gatsby asks Nick to invite Daisy to a tea party and Gatsby can just happen by and initiate a grand reunion. A few minutes before the appointed time, Gatsby is afraid Daisy will not show up. He even looks at his watch and claims that he does not have all day to wait for her (90), even though he was waited almost five years. Still, the more that time passes, the harder it is to recover the past, or so it seems to Gatsby.

Soon after Gatsby sees Daisy he accidentally knocks Nick's clock off the mantle (91). This shows his desire to stop the clock, even if it is an unconscious desire. But what Nick notes and what Gatsby fails to notice is that the clock did not break, and time goes on. When Gatsby feels as if the tea party is not going well, he dashes from the room and Nick follows. Nick scolds him for acting like a little boy (93). Also, Nick says later that Gatsby started to wind down like an overwound clock (97). Both of these demonstrate that Gatsby is regressing, both by becoming a child again in wanting to go back into the past, and by wanting to stop time in this past and keep his life in an arrested state. Further, Gatsby wishes to win back Daisy by taking her to see his wealth in his mansion. Nick says early in the book that Gatsby's mansion looks like the Hotel de Ville in

Normandy (9). Even his new wealth is kept in a place that looks old, a house with an inherent vision of the past.

The Last Waltz

The last party thrown by Gatsby is attended by Nick, Jordan, and the Buchanan's. This event is essential in understanding Gatsby's view of the past. Nick realizes that Gatsby wants Daisy to admit to Tom that she never loved him. In that confession she could obliterate the past three years of marriage, then Gatsby could marry Daisy back in Louisville in her parents' home just as if it were five years ago (116).

After Nick figures this out, he warns Gatsby that he cannot repeat the past, but Gatsby insists that he can (116). Gatsby's fixation with restoring the past is the Grail he has been pursuing in an attempt to cure his troubled heart, restore his seventeen-year-old platonic conception of self, and try to keep his life the way it was when he first kissed Daisy.

After insisting that he can repeat the past, Gatsby looks around him wildly, as if the past were lurking in the shadow of his house and just out of reach (116-117). While Gatsby feels one can repeat the past, he seems to know deep down how difficult it is. He then says that he'll fix everything just the way it was before (117). Notice Nick's commentary that follows: "He *talked a lot about the past* and I gathered that he wanted to *recover something*, some *idea of himself* perhaps, that had *gone into loving Daisy*. His life had been confused and disordered since then, but if he could once *return to a certain starting place* and go over it all slowly, he could find out what that thing was" (116-117, emp. mine – na). The very next paragraph tells of Gatsby and Daisy's first kiss and all of the weight that Gatsby attaches to it (117).

Look at how much is in these few lines. Gatsby is obsessed with restoring the past because in so doing he wishes to recover some idea about himself. In so doing he can return to a certain starting place, which for Gatsby is when he was seventeen and became Jay Gatsby. It is this notion of who had changed himself into that he put into loving Daisy. His Grail is to go back and become once again that person he was while at Fort Walker, a newly forged man who figured out how to cure the trouble in his heart. Interestingly, before he kisses Daisy he presumes that by kissing Daisy his mind would never romp, but it never says that it worked. Possibly it didn't and that might be why Gatsby is so enamored with the past because he wants a second chance at peace.

An interesting foil to Gatsby and his view of the past is Daisy. At this party she is afraid that some authentically radiant young girl might blot out the past five years of Gatsby's devotion to her with one fresh glance (115). While the past is a good thing for Gatsby, it's a bad thing for Daisy. She had known since the dinner party in late June that Gatsby was Nick's neighbor, and yet she never sought him out. It is not until the tea party and she learns of Gatsby's wealth that she is interested in him romantically again. That is because she loves money, not Gatsby. To Daisy, her past with Gatsby is not one she wishes to restore because it is a past with a poor Gatsby.

Consider how Gatsby's winning the Grail might heal Wilson. If Gatsby had been able to marry Daisy in the past, then Tom would not have ended up in New York. He only moved from Chicago to France to New York to escape the scandal of an affair. It seems Tom tries to escape his own past, too, and with just as little success. If Tom does not live in New York, Myrtle would not have been unfaithful to George, at least not with Tom. But Gatsby fails to recover the past, and incidentally George is wounded by it.

Gatsby's Failure To Obtain His Grail

I enjoy sports, and when the playoffs and championship games are on, then I try to watch as many of those as I can. But there is one thing I do not like about them. Inevitably, when a team wins a championship, the announcer says something stupid like this team has finally obtained that elusive Holy Grail. The Grail is not the prize at the end of a contest, nor is it the reward after a long journey, and it certainly isn't finally getting something you really want but hadn't been able to.

The Holy Grail is the apex of spiritual ascendancy and enlightenment. Obtaining the Grail is the only thing that can heal the moral corruption of the Waste Land. That is why Daisy Faye Buchannan is not the Grail in *The Great Gatsby*, even though Jay Gatsby is the Grail Knight. That would greatly cheapen the Grail to compare it to her. For Gatsby, the Grail is repeating the past, and in particular, to go back to a time before Daisy knew Tom so that he could marry her.

At The Plaza

The big showdown takes place in a room at the Plaza Hotel on one of the hottest days of that summer of '22. Earlier at lunch back at the Buchanan's, Tom had just learned of his wife's affair with Gatsby. The heat of the day mirrors the heat of the tension in the room. Gatsby tries to get Daisy to tell Tom that she never loved him (139). Notice, this is not just a declaration of whom she loves now, but whom she has loved and not loved all along.

Gatsby should have paid attention to Daisy's meaning when she referred to everyone's becoming older. When the music from the wedding below came up to the room, Daisy says that they should all dance, and the reason they don't is because they are getting old (135). She lets Gatsby knows that time marches on and no one can do anything about it.

Soon Gatsby insists to Tom that Daisy never loved her because she has been in love with him for the past five years. Finally Gatsby coerces Daisy to corroborate, but she quickly takes it back. She did once love Tom, but she loved Gatsby, too, adding a keen insistence that she cannot help what is past (140). These words seemed to bite into Gatsby physically, which shows that Gatsby is having a hard time wrapping his mind around the fact that he cannot repeat the past.

We learn from Nick's subsequent narrative that Daisy did wait for Gatsby, but eventually she began to move again with the seasons, and this means she started dating other men again (158). This culminates in dating and marrying Tom. Gatsby struggles to understand this and does not seem to be able to internalize it well. He vacillates from saying she never loved him to how she might have just for a minute when they were first married, but she still loved him, too (159-160).[xxiv] His Grail is gone and his reasons for hope have vanished, and still, Gatsby chases this ideal of having Daisy all to himself. This Daisy never loved Tom, or at least, not as deeply as she did Gatsby. As hard as he tries to hold on, a part of him recognizes that he has lost the freshest and best part of his relationship with Daisy (160-161).

The Apartment Party

One of the first scenes in the novel is the party at Tom and Myrtle's apartment. This takes place in the second chapter, which is just before the chapter with Gatsby's party. Fitzgerald stacks them to draw attention to how they foil each other. Gatsby's parties are part of his Grail pursuit, an effort to reverse and halt time. The party in the city is a testament to how time moves onward. There are many references to the forward progression of time at this party.

- Nick continually tells us the time of day
- Myrtle changes her dress a few times
- Myrtle's sister, Catherine, had someone last week look at her feet
- Mr. McKee in the past took a couple of pictures out on Long Island
- Mrs. McKee attended a party on West Egg a month ago
- Catherine went to Monte Carlo last year
- Catherine almost married a Jew some time in the past
- Myrtle talks about marrying George eleven years ago
- Tom opens a second bottle of whiskey
- Myrtle tells Nick how she met Tom and that she decides to start an affair with him because "you can't live forever"

To be clear, everything in the novel is a monument to the progression of time. Even Gatsby's effort to arrest time is based upon changes in his life as part of the forever moving clock that ticks for us all. It really doesn't matter how you perceive time, whether it is the constantly forward motion of events within history, or something more fluid that can best be called wibbly-wobbly, timey-wimey, you cannot repeat the past.

And still, we try. Gatsby has not tried anything that all of us readers have not wished to do, or possibly like Gatsby, tried and failed. All of us want to go back in time. We all want to go back to a simpler and purer era. The problem is that we desire to go back and live in what we think is a better time but with all of the wisdom of hindsight.

This is the real reason we cannot repeat the past. It really doesn't have anything to do with the immutable laws of the universe as much as from a practical sense of logic that tells us that you cannot relive the same experience. This is a hard lesson to learn, but one too many learn the hard way.

It's because this desire to repeat the past is so universal that so many writers tap into this same vein and write of people with the same agony as Jay Gatsby. Everyone from Shakespeare to Salinger has addressed this sentiment. So in the end, it doesn't matter if you are Romeo Montague or Holden Caulfield, or for that matter, Jay Gatsby, your mistakes have been written as a cautionary tale for all of your other brothers and sisters within humanity so that we will not follow you into a deep perdition of our own making.

So don't be too hard on our friend Mr. Gatsby. Too many critics are quite harsh, but they are only brave to speak out because they along with the other West Egg partiers are drunk on Gatsby's liquor. He's only done what all of us have wanted to do. It seems he just had the nerve to step out and act upon his compulsion, to live out his dream and take strides toward his hope. His simple tragedy reaffirms that you can't step in the same river twice.

Twentieth Century Novel As Twelfth Century Romance

While Grail literature covers near two millennia, a great concentration of books that codified much of our understanding of Arthurian legend were written in the twelfth century. Writers such as Chrétien de Troyes, Wolfram von Eisenbach, Marie de France, and Robert de Boron wrote Grail material in a literary form now referred to as Medieval Romance.

One of the standards of these Romances, and the Grail stories in particular, is the employment of Courtly Love. Since Fitzgerald uses Grail material in writing *The Great Gatsby*, it should not be a shock to see twelfth century Courtly Love in the novel, as well.[xxv]

Elements Of Courtly Love

The first scholar to identify Courtly Love was Gaston Paris in his article "Etudes sur les romans de la table ronde: Lancelot du Lac." C.S. Lewis developed this further in his book, *The Allegory Of Love*, particularly in his first chapter. Paris used the term Courtly Love, even though people in the twelfth century writers referred to the concept as *Amour Honestus*, which means "Honest Love," and *Fin*

Amor, which is "Refined Love." Paris identifies four rules common to Courtly Love.

> ➤ The relationship is extra-marital, and therefore illegitimate
> ➤ The male lover is inferior and insecure, while the female beloved is elevated, haughty, even despiteful
> ➤ The male lover can only earn beloved's affection by testing
> ➤ The passion is both art and science, subject to strict regulations

Marriage in the first half of the Dark Ages was more of a social, economic, and religious convention than a covenant based upon love. There was more feudal utility to it than anything else. Courtly Love came about to address genuinely human passions. The songs and poetry that praises Courtly Love speaks of a love that is more than outside of feudalism and Catholicism, but works against these outside forms. Courtly Love demands all of the devotion and adoration of Catholicism, as well as all of the structure and hierarchy of the economics of feudalism.

As with feudalism, the male lover serves as a vassal to his lord, which is his mistress. Similar to Catholicism, the penitent appeals to the Mother of God to intercede. But instead of praying to Mary plead to Christ, in Courtly Love petitions are made to Venus so that she might ask her son Cupid to act on behalf of the male lover.

Gatsby The Troubadour

I do not wish to go through all of the rules of courtly love, but there is one very applicable to this study. The courtly lover acts unreasonably because of his devotion, even insane. One of the clearest examples of this is one of the first Romances written, *Lancelot, the Knight Of The Cart*, by Chrétien de Troyes.

In the story, Guinevere is abducted and King Arthur sends his knights out to rescue her. Lancelot and Gawain find a man with a cart and asks him if he knows where the Queen was taken. He claims that he does and will show them if they get in his cart. Lancelot climbs in, but Gawain follows at a distance. Crazy people were taken to the most ancient of asylums in a cart, so this symbolizes how crazy in love Lancelot is, as well as Gawain's reluctance. As Lancelot fights for her release, he constantly looks behind him to see his Queen up in the window of a high tower. This means he is not paying attention to his adversary and is constantly being wounded.

We all know that love can make you crazy, and Gatsby is clearly in love. But he does so many things so unreasonable, one might think that he must insane. He builds his wealth through crime and thinks his wealth will impress Daisy. He throws wild summer parties hoping Daisy might come by. But probably the craziest thing Gatsby does is forcing the issue at the Plaza showdown. Tom even tells Gatsby "You're crazy" when he tells Tom that Daisy has always loved him and never loved Tom (138). These demonstrate Gatsby as a courtly lover.[xxvi]

Fitzgerald uses the moon as a symbol for the love Daisy and Gatsby share. In addition, the moon is a constant image for insanity. Our word "lunatic" comes from the Latin word for moon, *luna*. Gatsby acts like a lunatic in his pursuit of Daisy and Fitzgerald cements this as the constant lunar symbol of their love.

- ➤ When Nick first sees Gatsby, he stands in moonlight looking at green light (25)
- ➤ A premature moon hangs over Gatsby's party, which only exists to attract Daisy (47)
- ➤ Later Nick says that the moon had risen higher at the party (51)
- ➤ When Nick walks home from the party he looks back at Gatsby's house and says that a wafer of a moon shone over his house (60)

- On the day of the tea party Gatsby's dream becoming a reality had seemed as close as a star to the moon [which is only close in appearance, since stars are very far from our moon] (98)
- On the hottest day of the year as everyone heads for Manhattan and the Plaza Hotel, a silver curve of the moon hung in the western sky, even though it was still daytime (126)
- That night after Myrtle was killed, Nick notes that Gatsby's suit looked pink under the moon (150)
- When Nick leaves to go back home that night, he leaves Gatsby standing in the moonlight watching over nothing (153)
- After Gatsby's death and just before Nick leaves New York, he sees a profane word on the steps of Gatsby's mansion in the moonlight (188)

Nick & Tom

A good foil to Gatsby's elevated form of love for Daisy is Tom. While both have passion and physicality in their love for Daisy, Tom's love is merely *eros*, while Gatsby's love approaches *agape*. The contrasts of their ideas of love is seen in the Plaza Hotel room (137-138). Gatsby says he has loved Daisy for the past five years and she has loved him, even though she has not seen him since the October before he went to war. He loved her even though he was separated from her, and he asserts that she loved him in her mind all that time, as well.

Tom misunderstands and thinks Gatsby is claiming that they have been physically intimate for the entire time. That is because Tom's idea of love is diminished to nothing more than the sex act, whether it's with Daisy or Myrtle or someone else in Chicago or France with whom he had affairs. Tom never acts like he loves Daisy, or Myrtle, for that matter. He barely seems to even like them at times.

In a study of *The Great Gatsby* as a Grail Quest, it seems fitting that an analysis of the role of Courtly Love within the novel would be the final element considered. As is mentioned before, some of the most prominent works in the Arthurian canon were the twelfth century romances. This seems to tie in everything considered into a one final deposit of thought. There is one citation from the novel that brings in all of the elements mentioned in this section, and it is taken from Gatsby's youth soon after he ran away from home and labored to express this platonic form of himself that would take him from being James Gatz to Jay Gatsby. "But his heart was in a constant, ***turbulent riot***. The most grotesque and fantastic conceits haunted him in his bed at night. A ***universe of ineffable gaudiness*** spun itself out of his brain while the ***clock*** ticked on the wash-stand and the ***moon*** soaked with wet light his ***tangled clothes*** upon the floor" (105)

Endnotes

[i] All citations from the novel are taken from: F. Scott Fitzgerald, The Great Gatsby (New York: Simon & Schuster, 1925)

[ii] Nick may have "disapproved" of Gatsby "from beginning to end," Gatsby may have "represented everything" for which he has an "unaffected scorn," and Nick may even have "disliked him so much," but he comes down on his side. Gatsby, we are told, "turned out all right at the end" and his dream was "incorruptible" (Peter Lisca, "Nick Carraway And The Imagery Of Disorder" *Twentieth Century Literature*, April, 1967, 13.1, http://go.galegroup.com/ps/i.do?id=GALE%7CH1420003204&v=2.1&u=nysl_ me_garden&it=r&p=LitRC&sw=w&asid=067551bd91b379db649193ed702af4b 1)

[iii] More significantly, he (Nick) chooses to write the novel in such a way that we sense he is deliberately controlling our response (Lisca)

[iv] So why does he tell such an obvious lie, and why does Nick let it pass without comment? The only plausible explanation is that Gatsby wants Nick to know that he's lying, to show Nick that 'Gatsby' is a fictional creation. Nick's response of 'I see' implies that he is aware of the lie (he 'sees' the truth), but the fact that he neither challenges Gatsby nor points out the lie to the reader suggests that Nick chooses to be complicit with Gatsby's lies (Clair Stocks, "All Men Are (not] Created Equal," *The English Review*, February, 2007, 17.3, http://butlerlib.butlercc.edu:2390/ps/i.do?&id=GALE%7CA158832066&v=2.1 &u=klnb_bucc&it=r&p=LitRC&sw=w)

[v] Nick's manner of telling the story suggests that we should not be entirely convinced that he is giving us the 'truth' about Gatsby. He often gives what appear to be Gatsby's thoughts but are clearly imagined by himself. His narrative is peppered with phrases such as 'I suppose' and 'There must have been...' and words like 'possibly' and 'perhaps' that suggest that our response is not to Gatsby, but to Gatsby filtered through Nick's imagination (Lisca)

[vi] It seems clear from the San Francisco incident that Nick is not interested in exposing the real Gatsby. We are told in the first few pages that Nick enjoyed a brief period as an editor for the Yale News, and it seems that Nick's inclination towards editing may well extend to his account of Gatsby too. Nick wants to portray Gatsby as 'great' and to ignore or edit anything that might undermine that image. Indeed, towards the end of the novel, after Gatsby's death, Nick returns to his mansion to find 'an obscene word' scrawled on the step. Nick's reaction is to erase it, removing the word from the story as well as the step by not revealing it to the reader. As the story progresses, then, Nick's version seems increasingly unreliable as be glosses over lies, erases criticisms of Gatsby and avoids uncomfortable truths (Stocks)

[vii] To whatever degree Gatsby has won Nick over, he has won him not by an appeal to evidence but by an appeal to imagination. Because of his impressionability, Nick grasps an image and decks it out with his own bright feathers (Kent Cartwright, "Nick Carraway as an Unreliable Narrator," *Papers On Language And Literature*, 20.2, April 1984, Twentieth Century Literary Criticism. http://butlerlib.butlercc.edu:2390/ps/i.do?&id=GALE%7CH1420061753&v=2.1&u=klnb_bucc&it=r&p=LitRC&sw=w)

[viii] Surely, if Wilson had been brought to trial, the defense would have raised doubts that anybody would have been able to shoot Gatsby without puncturing the pneumatic mattress. This raises the possibility that Gatsby was killed and placed on the mattress afterwards, to float on the pool until someone found him (Anne Crow, *"The Great Gatsby* Mystery," *The English Review*, September, 2009, 20.1, http://butlerlib.butlercc.edu:2390/ps/i.do?&id=GALE%7CA208587501&v=2.1&u=klnb_bucc&it=r&p=LitRC&sw=w)

[ix] Clearly Nick is wrong to think 'It's all over now'. Obviously, Wolfshiem knows better, and his presence at the funeral might suggest a new line of enquiry for the inquest (Crow)

[x] Wolfshiem and Gatsby seem to be close friends and business associates. Wolfshiem tells Nick that '"We were so thick like that in everything"--he held up two bulbous fingers—"always together."' However, when Gatsby offers Nick 'a little business on the side', he reassures him that he 'wouldn't have to do any business with Wolfshiem'. Fitzgerald is suggesting that Gatsby may be branching out on his own. After Gatsby's death, Nick answers his phone and Slagle says 'Young Parke's in trouble ... They picked him up when he handed the bonds over the counter. They just got a circular from New York giving 'em the numbers just five minutes before.' If the police investigation is closing in on Gatsby's enterprises, then Wolfshiem might be worried that it will uncover some of his own activities (Crow)

[xi] Nick's final epiphany about Gatsby is contingent for its emergence on the act that precedes this epiphany: the repression or erasure of an "obscene word." In order for Gatsby to "turn out all right at the end," to come to "stand for America itself," his link to this word must be erased. Yet by foregrounding the process of this erasure, this "forgetting," Fitzgerald also seems to be problematizing the inevitability of the text's ending: Gatsby "turn(s) out all right" only if we forget, or repress, his obscenity (Barbara Will, "*The Great Gatsby* and the Obscene Word," *College Literature*, Fall 2005, 34.2, http://muse.jhu.edu/login?auth=0&type=summary&url=/journals/college_literature/v032/32.4will.html)

[xii] "Obscene," from the Latin "obscenaeus," meaning both "against the presentable" and "unrepresentable" (Will)

[xiii] Neither the advocate of a Christian origin, nor the Folklorist, can afford to ignore the arguments, and evidence of the opposing school, and while the result of half a century of patient investigation has been to show that the origin of the Grail story must be sought elsewhere than in ecclesiastical legend, or popular tale, I hold that the result has equally been to demonstrate that neither of these solutions should be ignored, but that the ultimate source must be sought for in a direction which shall do justice to what is sound in the claims of both (Jessie L. Weston, *From Ritual To Romance* (Cambridge, England: Cambridge University Press, 1920). http://sacred-texts.com/neu/frr/index.htm)

[xiv] Gatsby is, in fact, a contemporary Grail knight who undergoes numerous trials in order to become worthy of the precious object he desires (Barbara Tepa Lupack, "F. Scott Fitzgerald's 'Following of a Grail'." *Arthuriana*, Winter 1994, 4.4. 324-347. http://go.galegroup.com/ps/i.do?id=GALE%7CH1420054016&v=2.1&u=txshrpub100234&it=r&p=LitRC&sw=w)

[xv] (Kehl & Cooper also mention Auden's quest standards relative to *The Great Gatsby*)

[xvi] Gatsby's efforts are endowed with ritualism, a ceremonialism that renders his quest beatific (D. G. Kehl & Allene Cooper, "Sangria in the Sangreal: *The Great Gatsby* as Grail Quest" *Rocky Mountain Review of Language and Literature* 47.4 (1993): 203-217. http://go.galegroup.com/ps/start.do?p=LitRG&u=viva2_svcc)

[xvii] All he possesses--his collection of imported shirts, his toilet seat of pure gold, his swimming pool and hydroplane--are calculated to alter in Daisy's eyes the deficiency of his past. He passes this test but fails to restore the king and the Waste Land, perhaps because he does not ask the right question of the grail (Kehl & Cooper)

xviii The tea party with Daisy at Nick's house is a major test for Gatsby. Because he was not wealthy, Daisy had not waited for Gatsby to return from Europe to marry her. At the tea party and in the subsequent events, Gatsby attempts to retake the test he could not pass five years earlier (Kehl & Cooper)

xix If the Grail story be based upon a Life ritual the character of the Fisher King is of the very essence of the tale, and his title, so far from being meaningless, expresses, for those who are at pains to seek, the intention and object of the perplexing whole. The Fisher King is, as I suggested above, the very heart and centre of the whole mystery, and I contend that with an adequate interpretation of this enigmatic character the soundness of the theory providing such an interpretation may be held to be definitely proved (Weston)

xx The misfortunes of the land have been treated rather as an accident, than as an essential, of the Grail story, entirely subordinate in interest to the *dramatis personae* of the tale, or the objects, Lance and Grail, round which the action revolves. As a matter of fact I believe that the 'Waste Land' is really the very heart of our problem; a rightful appreciation of its position and significance will place us in possession of the clue which will lead us safely through the most bewildering mazes of the fully developed tale (Weston)

xxi Doctor T. J. Eckleberg, whose "persistent stare" presides over the "Waste Land" (24), is the Maimed King who corresponds to the Dead or Wounded God (Kehl & Cooper)

xxii Daisy is every bit as false, or fey, as her maiden name suggests. But that name, Fay, hints at more than her duplicity: it also suggests her kinship to another Fay, Morgan le Fay, the evil enchantress of Arthurian myth. Daisy's magic is as powerful, and as malicious, as her namesake's (Lupack)

xxiii It is during this orgiastic emptying of Gatsby's closets that the two achieve their greatest intimacy. Occurring in the bedroom of the great castle-like home he has purchased and maintained for her, this strange consummation of their relationship involves no actual lovemaking--fittingly so, perhaps, since Daisy represents for Gatsby a spiritual, not a physical ideal, and Gatsby represents for Daisy not the satisfaction of any sexual need but rather of her lust for material excess (Lupack)

xxiv Whereas Gatsby's humble origins prevented him from winning Daisy's hand years before, the ignoble past which haunts him again ruins his effort to claim her. The wealth he acquired through bootlegging and other illicit enterprises, rather than obliterating his low birth, gives him a history which Tom exploits, a history which Gatsby cannot ultimately explain or wish away, as he does with the five years of lost time apart from Daisy (Lupack)

[xxv] To earn Daisy's love, he observes a regimen as disciplined and purposeful as any knight errant's, transforming himself into what he believes she wants him to be (Lupack)

[xxvi] By pushing Daisy to repudiate Tom, Gatsby tries to legitimate his own unsacramental 'marriage' to her, which in his eyes invalidates her subsequent marriage to Tom (Lupack)

Made in the USA
Lexington, KY
15 May 2018